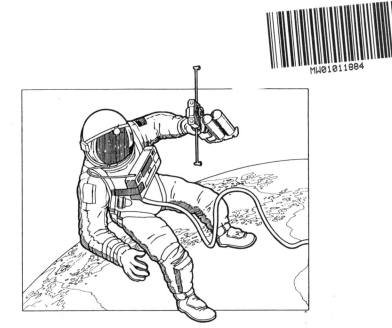

HISTORY OF
SPACE EXPLORATION
Coloring Book

Bruce LaFontaine

DOVER PUBLICATIONS, INC., New York

Bruce LaFontaine is an illustrator and writer living in Rochester, New York. He specializes in the subject areas of aviation and space technology, natural science, and history. He is a graduate of the State University of New York with a Bachelor's Degree in Drawing and Painting.

Published in Canada by General Publishing Company, Ltd.,
30 Lesmill Road, Don Mills, Toronto, Ontario.
Published in the United Kingdom by Constable and Company, Ltd.

History of Space Exploration Coloring Book is a new work,
first published by Dover Publications, Inc., in 1989.

DOVER *Pictorial Archive* SERIES

International Standard Book Number: 0-486-26152-2

Manufactured in the United States of America
Dover Publications, Inc.
31 East 2nd Street
Mineola, N.Y. 11501

INTRODUCTION

Imagine the rust-colored sand dunes of Mars, Saturn's giant moon Titan with its rivers and oceans of liquid methane, or the Sea of Tranquility where men from Earth first set foot on the lunar surface. These are some of the images in the history of space exploration. This history extends from classical times and is represented by two distinct lineages. First, there is the visionary tradition in literature, beginning with Lucian (c. 120–180) and continuing with Ariosto, Verne, and Wells. The other lineage is scientific and includes Copernicus, Galileo, Kepler, and Newton. These two traditions began to converge in the nineteenth century, most convincingly in the figure of Russian scientist Konstantin Tsiolkovsky, who was clearly influenced by Verne and Wells. For the first time, dreams of interplanetary travel were taken out of the realm of the purely fantastic with the development of theories of rocket propulsion and aerodynamics. The pioneering efforts of Tsiolkovsky, Oberth, and Goddard would inspire a later generation of engineers, technicians, and scientists to transform those theories into the reality of rockets and space vehicles. The story takes us from 1926, when the first liquid-fuel rocket reached an altitude of 184 feet, to the giant Saturn V that launched American astronauts on their 246,000-mile lunar landing mission in 1969.

The modern era of the space age began in 1957 with the launching of Sputnik, the world's first artificial satellite. Since then it has assumed the character of a race between the United States and the Soviet Union, competing to achieve the next historic space "first." We have gone from simple satellites like Sputnik and Explorer to complex communications satellites that now circle the globe, providing a network of worldwide communication. We have witnessed the journey of robot probes to the Moon and the planets Mars, Venus, and Jupiter, worlds that were once just pinpoints of light in the night sky but are now seen close-up in pictures taken by machines from Earth. Most importantly, the story of the space age is the story of men and women, astronauts and cosmonauts, who saw the challenge of exploration and accepted it with enthusiasm. From the first brief orbital flights of the Mercury and Vostok spacecraft to the landing of American astronauts on the Moon, the history of space exploration is the story of our ceaseless quest for new knowledge and new frontiers to explore.

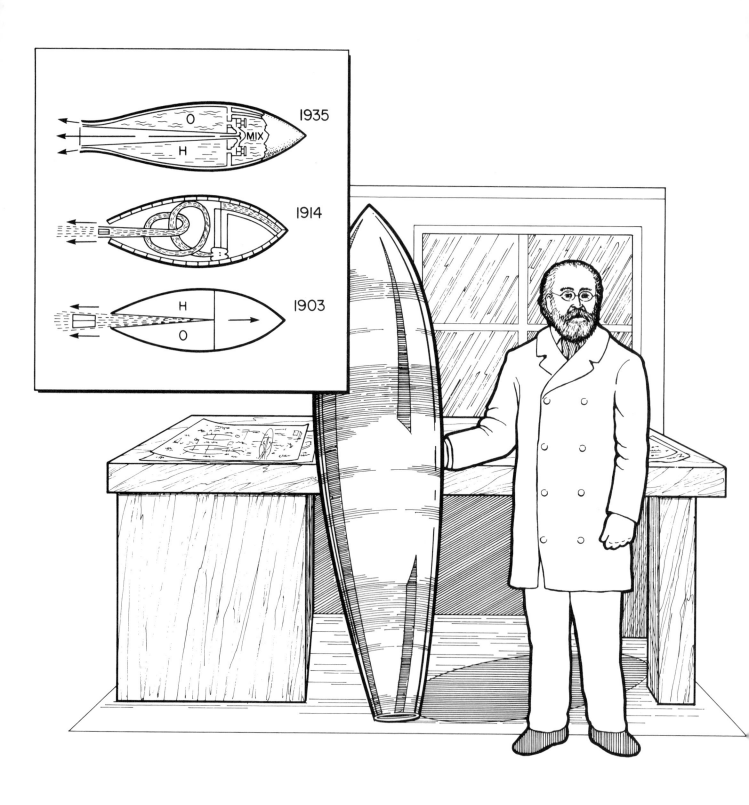

Konstantin Tsiolkovsky. One of the founding fathers of the Space Age was Konstantin Tsiolkovsky (1857–1935), born 150 miles southeast of Moscow. Deaf from the age of eight, he was self-educated and in his early life read and experimented on his own, eventually becoming a teacher of mathematics, chemistry, and physics. In 1887 he began to publish articles that described the basic laws of rocket propulsion and in 1903 wrote his most important book, *The Exploration of Space with Reactive Devices.* In this book he explained how rockets could be used to escape Earth's gravity and how multistage rockets could be used to achieve Earth orbit. He described how liquid oxygen and liquid hydrogen could be mixed and ignited, the exhaust being propelled from a nozzle at the back of a rocket to attain great speed and altitude. The power of modern rockets is given as the measure of this reaction in pounds (lbs.) of thrust. In later years, he went on to write of the possibility of space stations, satellites, solar energy, and the use of space suits. Inspired by writers like Jules Verne and H. G. Wells, Tsiolkovsky provided the first giant step from the fiction of space travel to its realization with his solid scientific theories.

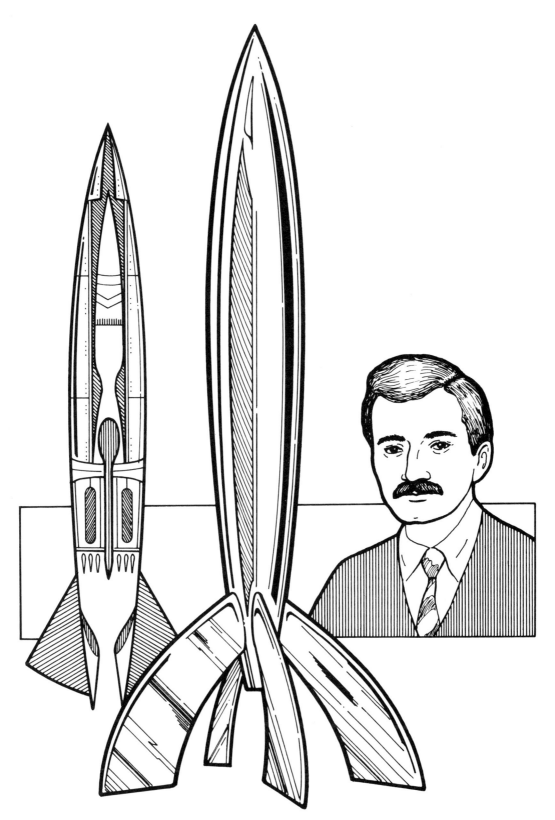

Hermann Oberth. Hermann Oberth was another early pioneer of space exploration. His books and articles did much to popularize the idea of space travel with the general public and, more importantly, to foster actual experimentation by scientists. He was born in Transylvania, Rumania, in 1894, educated in Germany, and, like Tsiolkovsky, became a teacher. His first book, published in 1923, was entitled *The Rocket into Interplanetary Space.* In it he theorized how rockets could launch payloads into space, described the design of a rocket, the Model B *(left),* and the propellants that could be used to power it. His second book, *The Road to Space Travel,* published in 1929, was widely read throughout Europe and America. The book was of great interest to scientists in Germany and inspired them to form the German Society for Space Travel in 1929 (the same year, Oberth worked on the model rocket, designed according to his theories, shown above as a promotion for a German science-fiction film). The Society was an organization of engineers, scientists, writers, and others interested in rocketry and space exploration. In other countries similar groups followed this example and formed the American Rocket Society, the British Interplanetary Society, and the Group for the Investigation of Reaction Motion in the Soviet Union.

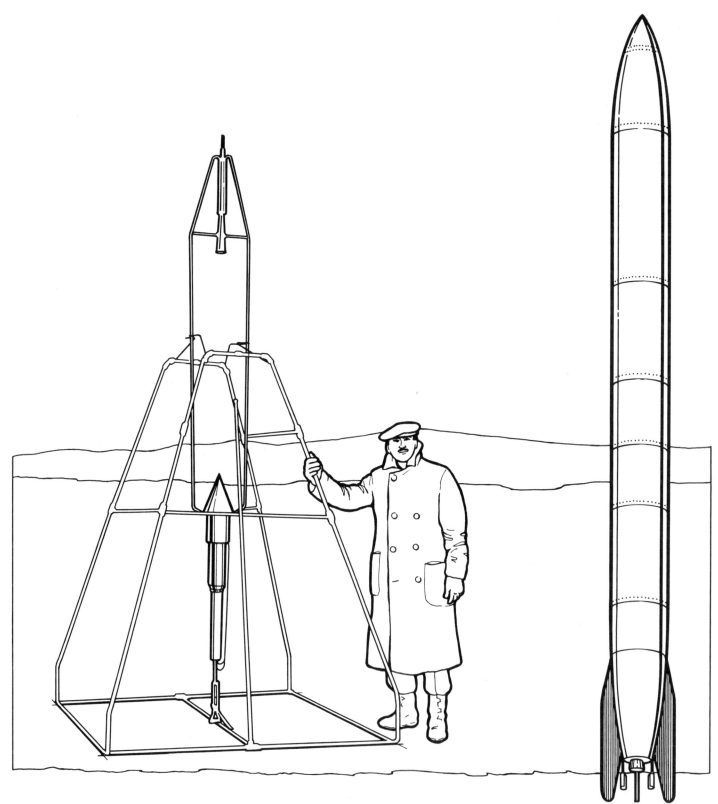

Robert Goddard. America's great astronautics pioneer, Dr. Robert H. Goddard was born in Worcester, Massachusetts, in 1882. As a boy he also was influenced toward rocketry by the stories of Jules Verne and H. G. Wells. While in high school he submitted an article to *Popular Science* magazine entitled "The Navigation of Space." He eventually received a doctorate degree in physics from, and began teaching at, Clark University in Worcester. While teaching, he conducted experiments with rockets and published his findings in 1919 under the title "A Method of Reaching Extreme Altitudes." On March 16, 1926, he successfully launched the world's first liquid-fuel rocket *(left)* from a field on a Massachusetts farm. It was 10 feet high and flew for 2½ seconds to an altitude of 184 feet. Through the next 15 years he continued to build and launch bigger, more complex rockets, culminating in his final design *(right)*, launched in 1941. It was 22 feet long and reached an altitude of 10,000 feet. It had all the components of modern rockets including gyroscopic stabilizers and turbine pumps for the liquid oxygen fuel.

After Goddard's death in 1945, he was recognized as having provided the foundation of modern rocket science. The National Aeronautics and Space Administration (NASA) named its Goddard Space Flight Center in Maryland in his honor.

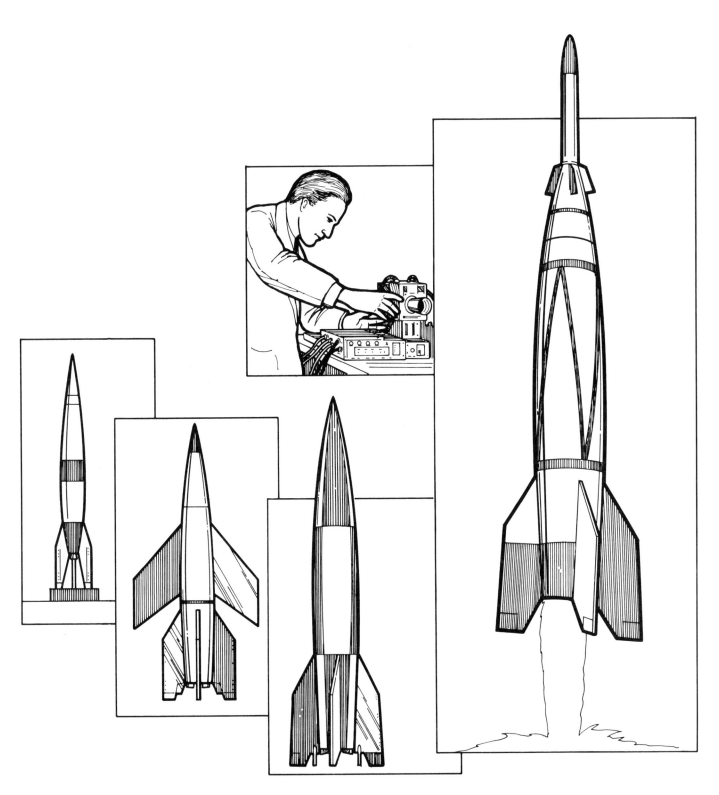

Wernher von Braun. During World War II German scientists developed a series of rockets with great range and payload capacity. First among these was the A-3 *(left)*, 21 feet long, with a thrust of 3,300 lbs. By 1943 its successor, the A-4, later renamed the V-2 *(second from right)*, was launched. It was a powerful and complex rocket, the forerunner of the spacecraft boosters built by the U.S. and the U.S.S.R. in the 1950s and 60s. The V-2 was 46 feet long and weighed 27,000 lbs. It could carry a 2,000-lb. warhead a distance of 200 miles and reach 3,600 miles per hour (mph), a speed far in excess of any other rocket or aircraft of that time. A winged version, the A-4b, was also developed *(second from left)*.

The Nazi war effort began to collapse in 1945 and many German rocket scientists defected to the U.S. Army. Most important among these was Dr. Wernher von Braun (1912–1977), who had been the civilian scientist in charge of the V-2 program. He led the American rocket development program from the late 1940s through the 1960s. Another group of German experts was captured by the Soviet army and became the core group that developed the rockets that launched Sputnik and other spacecraft. In 1949 the team led by Dr. von Braun launched an American modified V-2/WAC Corporal *(right)* to a record altitude of 244 miles, well into what is officially designated as "outer space."

Dr. von Braun's contributions to the American space program were enormous. In 1975 he was awarded the National Medal of Science, the nation's highest scientific honor.

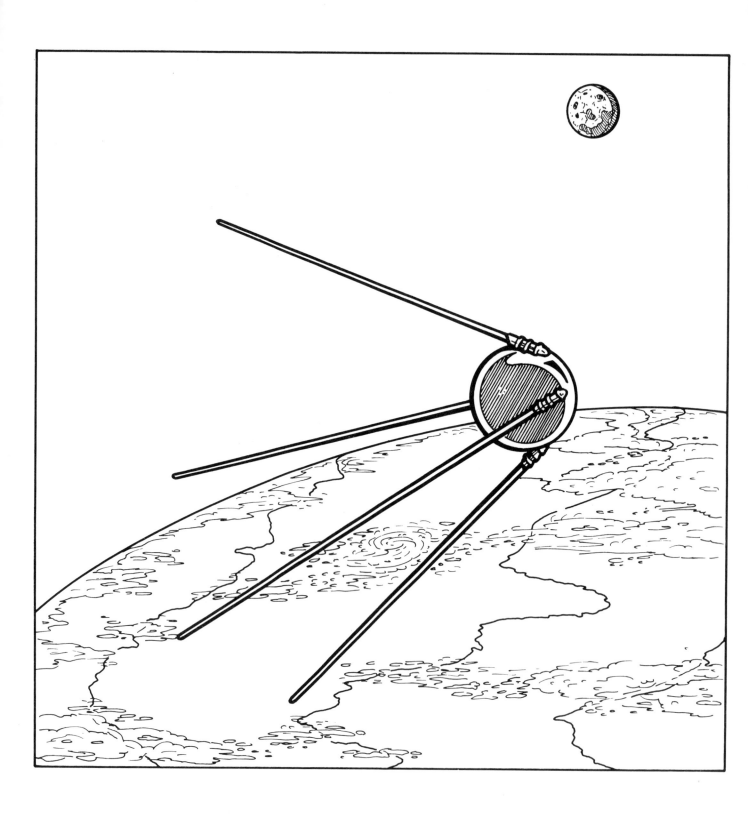

Sputnik 1. The "beep-beep-beep" of a radio signal from space announced the official start of the space race and showed that the Soviet Union had taken the lead. On October 4, 1957, the world was amazed by news that the Soviets had launched the world's first artificial satellite, Sputnik 1 (Sputnik means "fellow traveler"). Sputnik 1 was a globe-shaped instrument 23 inches in diameter and weighing 185 lbs. It was launched into orbit by a multistage rocket booster, the A-1/SL-3, that was a modified Soviet intercontinental ballistic missile. Its orbit ranged in altitude from 140 miles to 580 miles and it circled the Earth once every 96 minutes at a speed of 18,000 mph. On board it carried instruments to study the density and temperature of the upper atmosphere. By today's standards Sputnik was a very simple device, but its real importance lay in generating enormous activity and interest in the American space program, which would shortly enter the race with its own satellite.

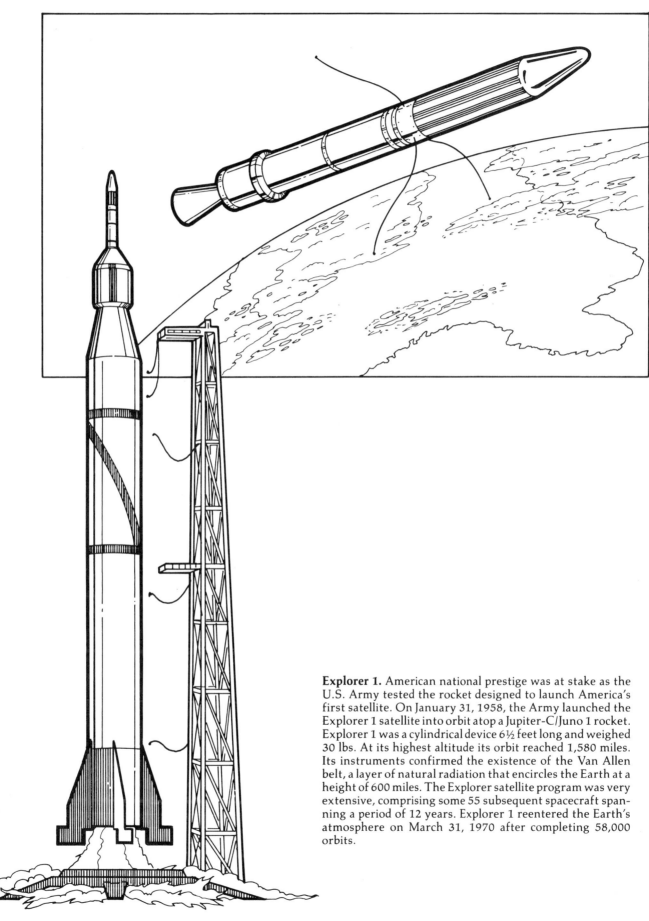

Explorer 1. American national prestige was at stake as the U.S. Army tested the rocket designed to launch America's first satellite. On January 31, 1958, the Army launched the Explorer 1 satellite into orbit atop a Jupiter-C/Juno 1 rocket. Explorer 1 was a cylindrical device 6½ feet long and weighed 30 lbs. At its highest altitude its orbit reached 1,580 miles. Its instruments confirmed the existence of the Van Allen belt, a layer of natural radiation that encircles the Earth at a height of 600 miles. The Explorer satellite program was very extensive, comprising some 55 subsequent spacecraft spanning a period of 12 years. Explorer 1 reentered the Earth's atmosphere on March 31, 1970 after completing 58,000 orbits.

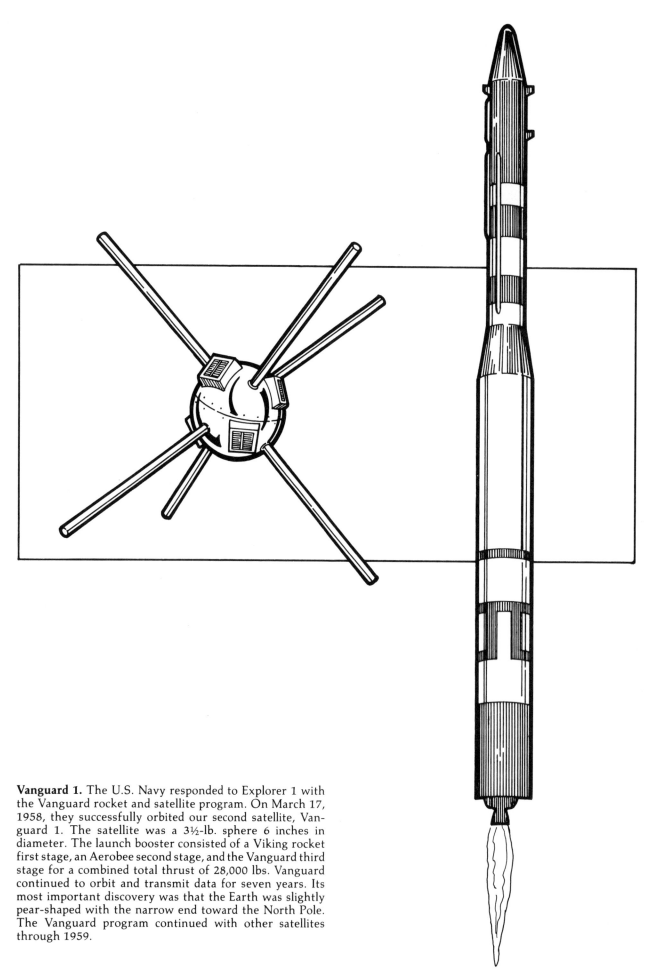

Vanguard 1. The U.S. Navy responded to Explorer 1 with the Vanguard rocket and satellite program. On March 17, 1958, they successfully orbited our second satellite, Vanguard 1. The satellite was a 3½-lb. sphere 6 inches in diameter. The launch booster consisted of a Viking rocket first stage, an Aerobee second stage, and the Vanguard third stage for a combined total thrust of 28,000 lbs. Vanguard continued to orbit and transmit data for seven years. Its most important discovery was that the Earth was slightly pear-shaped with the narrow end toward the North Pole. The Vanguard program continued with other satellites through 1959.

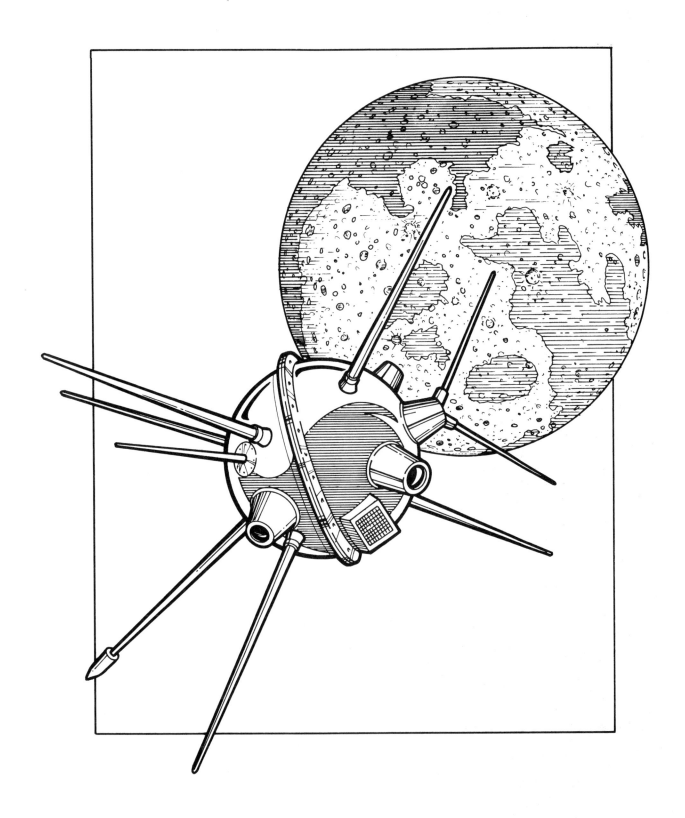

Luna 2. Beginning in 1959, the Soviet Union launched a series of lunar probes designed to orbit, photograph, and land on the Moon. One of these probes, Luna 2, became the first man-made object to impact on the lunar surface. Launched on September 12, 1959, the 860-lb. ball-shaped space probe carried instruments designed to study the Earth's radiation and magnetic field, cosmic rays, micro-meteors in space and the magnetic field of the Moon. On September 14, 34 hours after it was launched, radio signals from Luna 2 stopped, indicating that it had crashed on the lunar surface. The probe had impacted in the center of the Moon as seen from Earth, between the craters of Archimedes, Aristillus, and Autolycus.

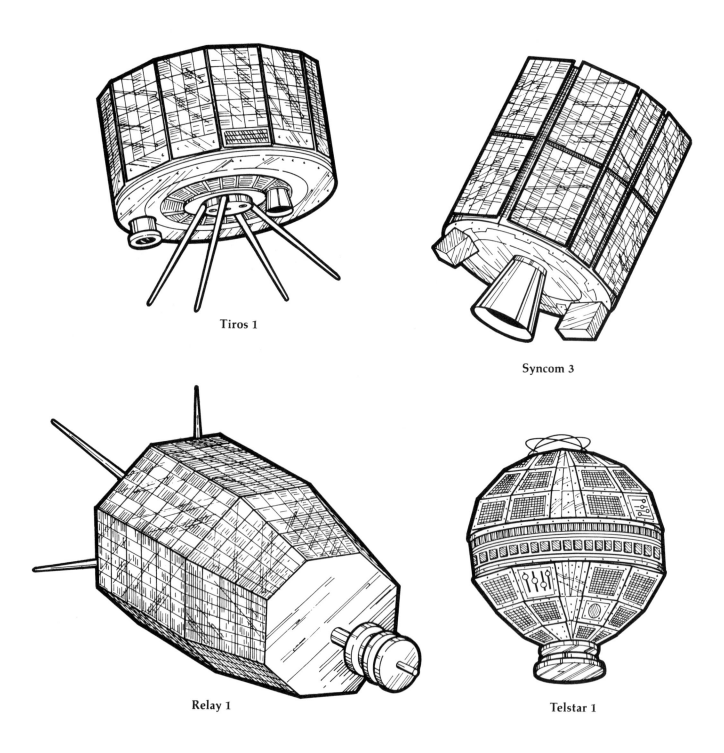

Tiros 1

Syncom 3

Relay 1

Telstar 1

Tiros 1, Telstar 1, Relay 1, and Syncom 3. In 1960 the United States launched the world's first weather-tracking satellite, Tiros 1 *(upper left)*. It was 42 inches long and 19 inches high, and weighed 280 lbs. Its outside surface was covered with solar cells to convert sunlight into electrical power. It had two TV cameras that photographed weather patterns on Earth. During its 89 days in orbit it transmitted over 22,000 photographs back to Earth. In 1962 a breakthrough in communications satellites, Telstar 1 *(lower right)*, was launched. It was carried into an elliptical orbit that ranged in altitude from 600 to 3,500 miles. Telstar provided the first live television pictures broadcast from one continent to another. It was the forerunner of our current global satellite communications network. Another important satellite launched in 1962 was Relay 1 *(lower left)*, designed to transmit voice and TV pictures between continents and linked to stations in the U.S., Europe, Japan, and Brazil. In 1964 the Syncom 3 satellite *(upper right)* was launched into a geosynchronous orbit (synchronized with the Earth's rotation). At an altitude of 22,300 miles in space, it always remains in the same position in relation to the planet below. The geosynchronous satellite system permits the instantaneous broadcast of TV and radio across the entire surface of the Earth.

Ham the Astrochimp. The next step in the American space program would be a manned suborbital flight in the Mercury one-man space capsule. Before a man could be launched into space, however, flight testing of the rocket and Mercury capsule had to be successfully accomplished. In order to measure human physical response to the tremendous acceleration, or G-force, of blast-off and reentry a chimpanzee was chosen to make a first flight. On January 31, 1961, a chimpanzee named Ham became our first "astrochimp." He was launched into suborbital space for a 16½-minute flight and recovered unharmed 422 miles downrange from Cape Canaveral. His capsule reached a speed of 4,280 mph and proved spaceworthy, as did the Redstone rocket booster. Ham's flight helped pave the way for America's first man in space, Alan B. Shepard, whose flight would soon follow.

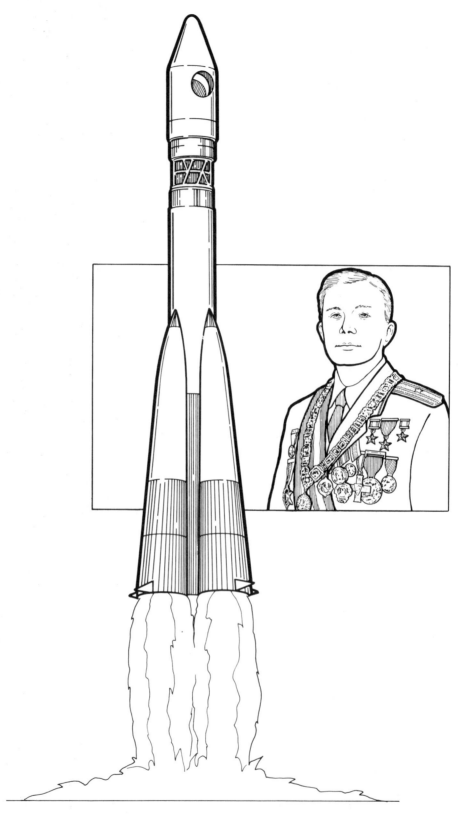

Yuri Gagarin and Vostok 1. In 1961 the Soviet Union achieved a historic milestone in the exploration of space. On April 12, Soviet Air Force Major Yuri Gagarin became the first man to enter space and orbit the Earth. He was carried into space in a Vostok space capsule launched by an A-1/SL-3 rocket. The A-1/SL-3 booster accelerated him to the necessary orbital speed of 17,500 mph on a flight that lasted 108 minutes. His single orbit reached a maximum altitude of 187 miles and at its lowest point was 109 miles above the Earth's surface. The Vostok (meaning "east") spacecraft was a ball-shaped capsule 7½ feet in diameter with a power and life-support module attached that had a total weight of 10,000 lbs. At the end of his first orbit Gagarin fired his retro-rockets to slow his speed for reentry into the atmosphere. At a height of 22,000 feet an ejection seat propelled him from the capsule and he parachuted to earth in his orange spacesuit. The Vostok capsule landed separately several miles away.

Yuri Gagarin died in a plane crash in 1968 while training for another space mission. In the Soviet Union he is considered one of its greatest heroes and will be remembered everywhere as the first man in space.

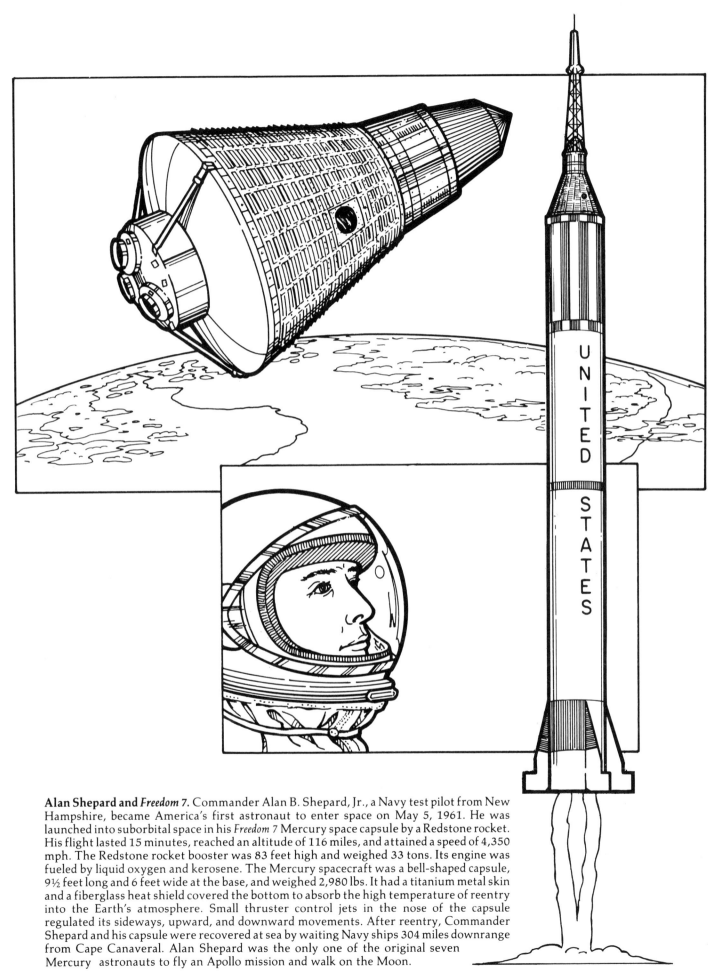

Alan Shepard and *Freedom 7.* Commander Alan B. Shepard, Jr., a Navy test pilot from New Hampshire, became America's first astronaut to enter space on May 5, 1961. He was launched into suborbital space in his *Freedom 7* Mercury space capsule by a Redstone rocket. His flight lasted 15 minutes, reached an altitude of 116 miles, and attained a speed of 4,350 mph. The Redstone rocket booster was 83 feet high and weighed 33 tons. Its engine was fueled by liquid oxygen and kerosene. The Mercury spacecraft was a bell-shaped capsule, 9½ feet long and 6 feet wide at the base, and weighed 2,980 lbs. It had a titanium metal skin and a fiberglass heat shield covered the bottom to absorb the high temperature of reentry into the Earth's atmosphere. Small thruster control jets in the nose of the capsule regulated its sideways, upward, and downward movements. After reentry, Commander Shepard and his capsule were recovered at sea by waiting Navy ships 304 miles downrange from Cape Canaveral. Alan Shepard was the only one of the original seven Mercury astronauts to fly an Apollo mission and walk on the Moon.

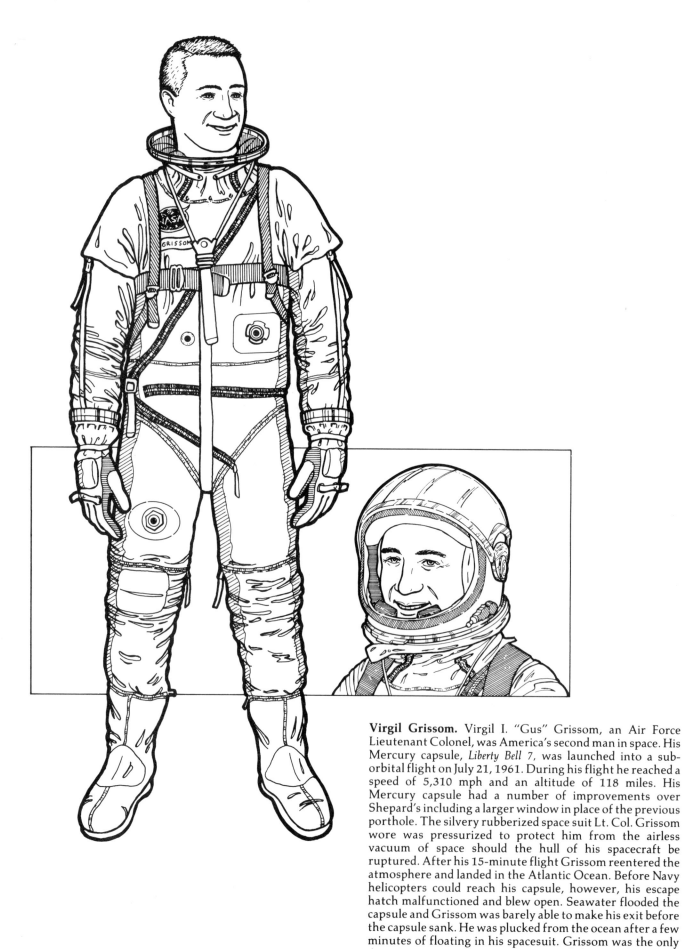

Virgil Grissom. Virgil I. "Gus" Grissom, an Air Force Lieutenant Colonel, was America's second man in space. His Mercury capsule, *Liberty Bell 7*, was launched into a suborbital flight on July 21, 1961. During his flight he reached a speed of 5,310 mph and an altitude of 118 miles. His Mercury capsule had a number of improvements over Shepard's including a larger window in place of the previous porthole. The silvery rubberized space suit Lt. Col. Grissom wore was pressurized to protect him from the airless vacuum of space should the hull of his spacecraft be ruptured. After his 15-minute flight Grissom reentered the atmosphere and landed in the Atlantic Ocean. Before Navy helicopters could reach his capsule, however, his escape hatch malfunctioned and blew open. Seawater flooded the capsule and Grissom was barely able to make his exit before the capsule sank. He was plucked from the ocean after a few minutes of floating in his spacesuit. Grissom was the only American astronaut to participate in all three of the American manned space programs: Mercury, Gemini, and Apollo.

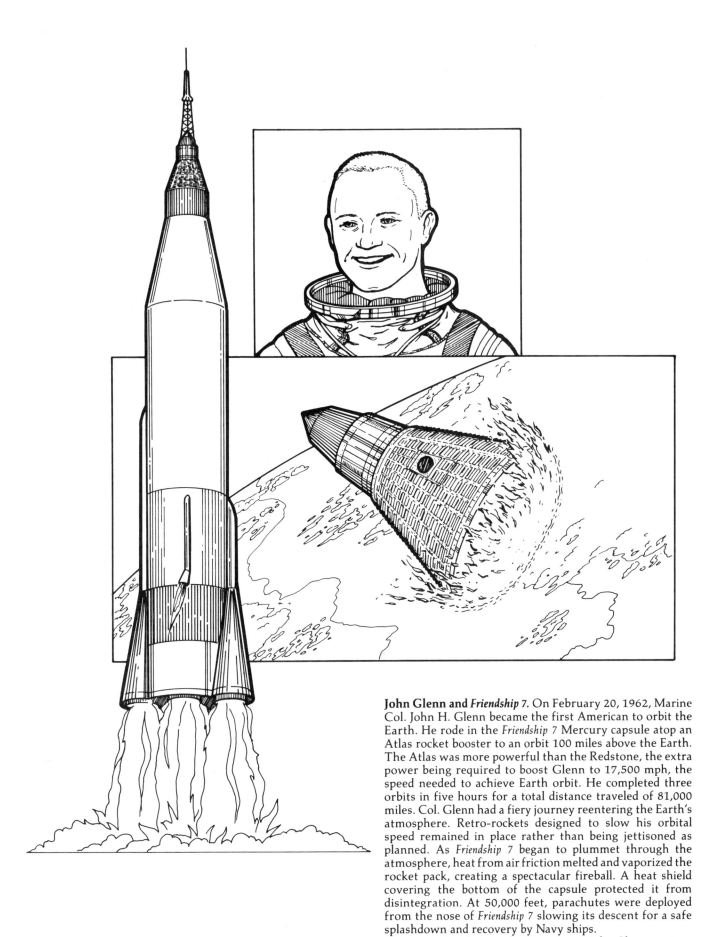

John Glenn and *Friendship 7.* On February 20, 1962, Marine Col. John H. Glenn became the first American to orbit the Earth. He rode in the *Friendship 7* Mercury capsule atop an Atlas rocket booster to an orbit 100 miles above the Earth. The Atlas was more powerful than the Redstone, the extra power being required to boost Glenn to 17,500 mph, the speed needed to achieve Earth orbit. He completed three orbits in five hours for a total distance traveled of 81,000 miles. Col. Glenn had a fiery journey reentering the Earth's atmosphere. Retro-rockets designed to slow his orbital speed remained in place rather than being jettisoned as planned. As *Friendship 7* began to plummet through the atmosphere, heat from air friction melted and vaporized the rocket pack, creating a spectacular fireball. A heat shield covering the bottom of the capsule protected it from disintegration. At 50,000 feet, parachutes were deployed from the nose of *Friendship 7* slowing its descent for a safe splashdown and recovery by Navy ships.

An American hero and space pioneer, John Glenn went on to a distinguished career as a United States Senator from Ohio.

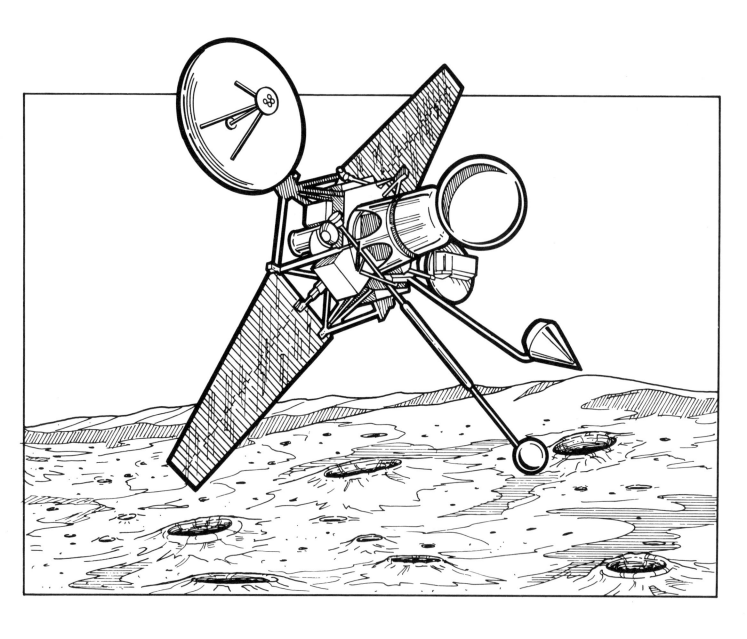

Ranger 4. The major goal of the U.S. space program was stated by President John F. Kennedy in 1961, "By the end of the decade, to land a man on the Moon and return him safely." To accomplish this task, unmanned robotic probes were designed and launched to test equipment and flight trajectories, and photograph possible lunar landing sites. The first of these probes was the Ranger series of space- craft. The Rangers were 13 feet long, weighed 700 lbs., and were equipped with television cameras. One of these probes, Ranger 4, became the first American spacecraft to reach the Moon when it crashed on the surface in April 1962. Later Ranger probes relayed over 17,000 TV pictures of the Moon and were essential in preparing for the Apollo manned lunar missions.

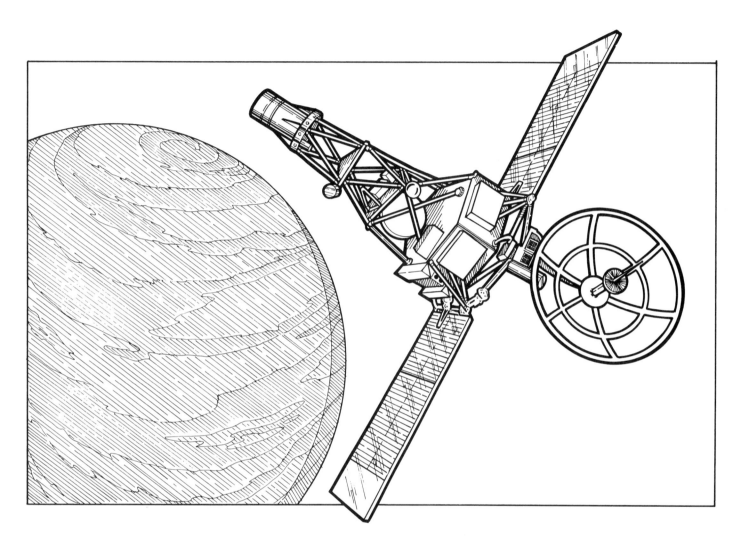

Mariner 2 Venus Probe. Exploration of neighboring planets has been one of the main goals of both the American and Soviet space programs. Because of the immense distances between the planets, unmanned robot probes have been sent on voyages of discovery throughout our Solar System. America's first successful planetary explorer was the Mariner 2 Venus probe, launched on August 27, 1962, by an Atlas Agena rocket. The 447-lb. spacecraft was 11 feet high and 16 feet across with its solar power panels extended. Venus lies an average distance of 30 million miles from Earth and Mariner 2's journey took 108 days. On December 14, 1962, the spacecraft passed within 21,594 miles of the planet. Mariner 2's instruments found that the surface temperature of Venus is over 800 degrees F., hot enough to melt lead. The atmosphere is a mix of deadly carbon dioxide and corrosive sulfuric acid. Venus seems to be a good example of the "greenhouse effect" whereby the sun's heat is trapped in the atmosphere, and radiated back onto the planet's surface, creating a nightmarish world of extreme heat and pressure. Mariner 2 also discovered that, unlike Earth, Venus has no magnetic field or radiation belt encircling it.

L. Gordon Cooper and *Faith 7.* The last American astronaut in the Mercury program was L. Gordon "Gordo" Cooper, Jr., an Air Force test pilot. He was launched into orbit on May 15, 1963, and spent 35 hours in *Faith 7,* his Mercury capsule. One of the purposes of Cooper's day-and-a-half-long mission was to test the human body's reaction to prolonged periods of weightlessness. Although he lost 10 lbs. during the flight he proved there were no lasting side effects from being in space for that length of time. Shortly before Cooper was to begin reentry, he lost all electrical power to his automatic control system. He was forced to take manual control of his spacecraft during the wild, buffeting ride back to Earth. His test-pilot skills served him well as he landed in the ocean just four miles from the waiting recovery ship. Cooper traveled a distance of 600,000 miles during his 22-orbit mission and holds the American solo spaceflight duration record.

The first group of astronauts in the Mercury program had proved it was possible to launch a man into Earth orbit and return him safely. The American space program now focused on the next step, the two-man Gemini spacecraft.

Vostok 5. The Soviet Vostok spacecraft was the equivalent to the American Mercury capsule. It consisted of a thick-walled spherical chamber for the cosmonaut and a power and life-support section attached at the rear. Together they measured 14 feet long and 8 feet in diameter, and weighed 10,400 lbs., twice the weight of the Mercury capsule. Vostok 5 was equipped with an ejection seat for the pilot to parachute to Earth separately if he encountered landing difficulties. The rocket that boosted the spaceship into orbit was the A-1/SL-3 Vostok (three times as powerful as the Mercury-Atlas rocket). It was constructed around a central core with four engines and had four strap-on boosters, each of them with four engines.

On June 14, 1963, Vostok 5 was launched with cosmonaut Valery Bykovsky. He was a twenty-eight-year-old Soviet Air Force pilot who had trained with Yuri Gagarin in the first group of Soviet cosmonauts. Bykovsky was to set a solo spaceflight endurance record that still stands. He completed 81 orbits over a four-day period. The Vostok program would be superseded in 1964 by the larger three-man Voskhod spacecraft.

Valentina Tereshkova and Vostok 6. The last in the Vostok series of space missions was another historic event in the Soviet space program. On board the Vostok 6 capsule was cosmonaut Valentina Tereshkova, the first woman to enter space and orbit the Earth. Valentina was a twenty-six-year-old former cotton-mill worker and amateur parachute jumper who was selected for training as a cosmonaut. She was launched on June 16, 1963, two days after the launch of

Vostok 5 with Valery Bykovsky. With two spacecraft in orbit at the same time, the Soviets had scored another first. At one point the cosmonauts were within three miles of each other. Nineteen years would pass before the next woman would enter space, cosmonaut Svetlana Savitskaya, who would be followed a year later by American astronaut Sally Ride.

Mariner Mars Probes. The Mariner robot explorers sent to Mars began with the voyage of Mariner 4 in November 1964. The journey took 9 months and covered 325 million miles, bringing it to a flyby of the planet in July of 1965 at a distance of 6,118 miles. It had color TV cameras to send pictures back to Earth. Mariner 4 found Mars to be a windswept desert planet, heavily cratered, with a thin atmosphere (1/100 the density of Earth's) composed mainly of carbon dioxide.

In March 1969 Mariners 6 and 7 flew by Mars at an altitude of 2,120 miles. They discovered the largest mountain in the solar system, an extinct volcano named Mt. Olympus *(shown here)* that towers 80,000 feet above the Martian plains and is over 250 miles wide at the base. They photographed a Martian "Grand Canyon," since named Valley of the Mariners, over 3,000 miles long and 300 miles wide with cliff walls soaring 30,000 feet high.

In 1971 Mariner 9 encountered Mars and found the entire planet shrouded in a dust storm. After a few weeks the storm cleared and Mariner 9 began taking photos. Orbiting Mars for the next 329 days, Mariner took 7,329 pictures, mapping over 90% of the surface. It found that the planet has two distinct hemispheres: the south, an ancient, heavily cratered landscape, and the north, a geologically younger series of plains, extinct volcanoes, canyons, lava flows, and dry river beds.

height in feet

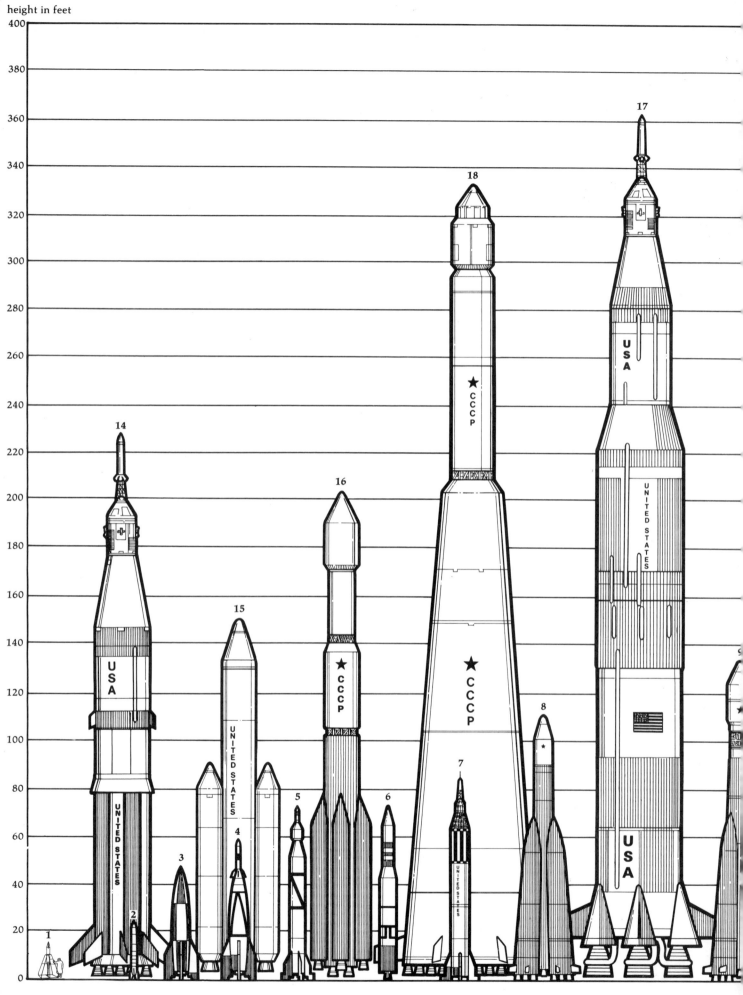

24

Rocket Launch Vehicle Comparison Chart, 1926–1987.
Data presented as follows: date, nationality and/or name of rocket, power in pounds of thrust, and principal payload.

(1) 1926—First liquid-fuel rocket, launched by American Dr. Robert Goddard—power not measured—no payload; flight duration 2.5 seconds, altitude 184 feet.

(2) 1941—Final rocket launched by Dr. Goddard—985 lbs.—altitude-measuring instrumentation.

(3) 1944—German V2—55,000 lbs.—2000-lb. explosive warhead.

(4) 1949—American V2 WAC/Corporal—56,000 lbs.—high-altitude research instrumentation.

(5) 1958—American Jupiter-C/Juno 1—83,000 lbs.—first American Earth satellite, Explorer 1.

(6) 1958—American Vanguard—28,000 lbs.—second American satellite, Vanguard 1.

(7) 1961—American Redstone—78,000 lbs.—Mercury capsule with first American astronaut into suborbital space.

(8) 1957—Soviet A-1/SL-3 Sputnik Booster—988,000 lbs.—first Earth satellite, Sputnik 1.

(9) 1961—Soviet A-1/SL-3 Vostok Booster—996,000 lbs.—Vostok capsule with first man to orbit the Earth.

(10) 1962—American Atlas—360,000 lbs.—Mercury capsule with first American to orbit the Earth.

(11) 1962—American Atlas-Centaur—389,000 lbs.—Surveyor 1, unmanned lunar probe.

(12) 1963—Soviet A-2/SL-4—1,460,000 lbs.—first Voskhod (3-man) capsule, subsequent Soyuz spacecraft.

(13) 1965—American Titan II—430,000 lbs.—Gemini (2-man) space capsule.

(14) 1966—American Saturn 1B—1,656,000 lbs.—Apollo 5 and 7 spacecraft to Earth orbit in preparation for Lunar flights.

(15) 1965—American Titan IIIC—2,360,000 lbs.—military and civilian satellites.

(16) 1965—Soviet D-1-h/SL-12 Proton Booster—3,500,000 lbs.—Salyut space station, unmanned planetary probes.

(17) 1967—American Saturn V—7,750,000 lbs.—Apollo lunar landing flights, Skylab space station.

(18) 1967—Soviet G-1-e Booster—10,000,000 lbs.+—Proposed manned lunar landing and 12-person space station (both canceled).

(19) 1974—American Titan IIIE—2,361,000 lbs.—Viking Mars landers, Mariner Venus and Mercury probes.

(20) 1981—American Space Shuttle—6,425,000 lbs.—satellites, Hubbell space telescope, U.S. space-station components, planetary probes.

(21) 1982—American Delta 3920—766,000 lbs.—satellites.

(22) 1982—American Titan 34D—2,498,000 lbs.—satellites.

(23) 1987—Soviet Energia SL-17 booster—6–8,000,000 lbs.—Mir space-station components, future Soviet Buran ("Snowstorm") unpowered space shuttle.

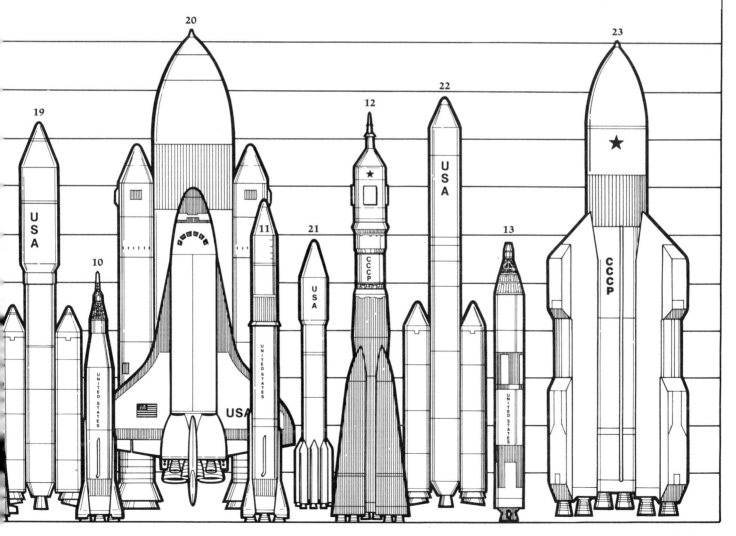

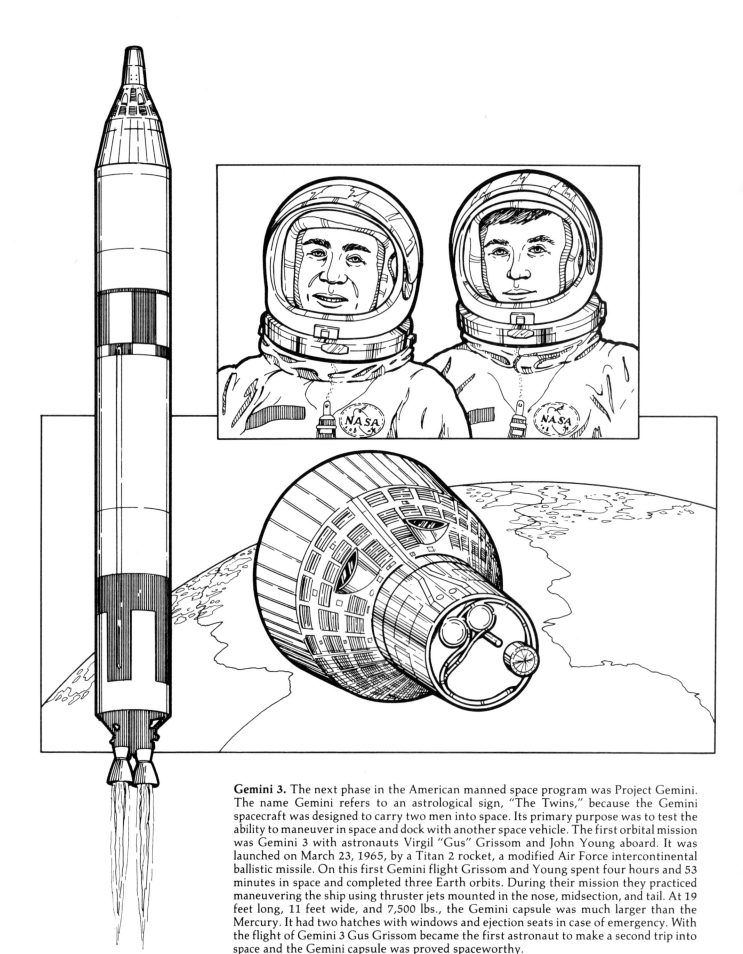

Gemini 3. The next phase in the American manned space program was Project Gemini. The name Gemini refers to an astrological sign, "The Twins," because the Gemini spacecraft was designed to carry two men into space. Its primary purpose was to test the ability to maneuver in space and dock with another space vehicle. The first orbital mission was Gemini 3 with astronauts Virgil "Gus" Grissom and John Young aboard. It was launched on March 23, 1965, by a Titan 2 rocket, a modified Air Force intercontinental ballistic missile. On this first Gemini flight Grissom and Young spent four hours and 53 minutes in space and completed three Earth orbits. During their mission they practiced maneuvering the ship using thruster jets mounted in the nose, midsection, and tail. At 19 feet long, 11 feet wide, and 7,500 lbs., the Gemini capsule was much larger than the Mercury. It had two hatches with windows and ejection seats in case of emergency. With the flight of Gemini 3 Gus Grissom became the first astronaut to make a second trip into space and the Gemini capsule was proved spaceworthy.

Gemini 4. Edward H. White was the first American astronaut to "walk in space." On June 3, 1965, he stepped from the open hatch of his Gemini 4 spacecraft and floated weightlessly in Earth orbit. He was connected to the Gemini capsule by a 25-foot gold-plated nylon line. Using a hand-held compressed-gas maneuvering gun, he was able to propel himself about. The spacesuit he wore was con- structed with 22 different layers designed for protection from extremes of heat and cold, cosmic rays, and penetra- tion by micrometeors. During his 21 minutes in space he traveled the distance from Hawaii to Bermuda, about 6,000 miles. Ed White's historic space walk was an important test of the ability of astronauts to work in outer space.

Gemini 5. On August 17, 1965 Gemini 5 was launched with astronauts Gordon Cooper and Charles "Pete" Conrad on board. Gemini 5 established a new space-flight endurance record for that time by staying in space for seven days and 22 hours and completing 120 orbits. The flight duration was the same as that of the planned Apollo lunar mission and was useful for testing spacecraft systems and crew endurance for that length of time.

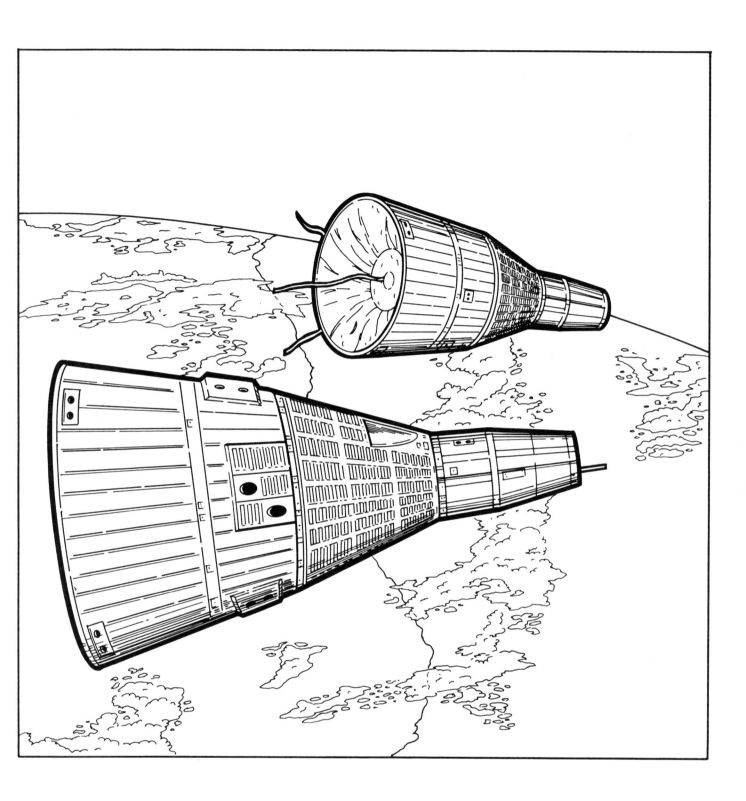

Gemini 6 and 7. Gemini 6 and 7 were the first spacecraft to achieve a rendezvous in Earth orbit. This was a crucial step in preparing for the upcoming Apollo Moon-landing mission. First to be launched—on December 4, 1965—was Gemini 7 with astronauts Frank Borman and James Lovell. They would act as the target vehicle for the rendezvous with Gemini 6. On December 15, 1965, Gemini 6 was launched with Wally Schirra and Thomas Stafford on board. The two spacecraft located one another, maneuvering as close as one foot apart, and orbited the Earth together for five hours and 18 minutes while traveling at a speed of over 17,500 mph. Gemini 6 returned to Earth after three orbits and one day in space but Gemini 7 stayed aloft, breaking the space-flight endurance record with 206 orbits over a 13-day period. The Gemini program ended with Gemini 12 in 1966 but had proved invaluable in preparing astronauts for the Apollo flights that would soon take place.

Surveyor 1. Next in the American program of unmanned lunar probes was the Surveyor series of spacecraft. These were designed to soft-land on the surface of the Moon while scouting out possible landing sites for the upcoming Apollo manned flights. On May 30, 1966, Surveyor 1 was launched on its Moon voyage by an Atlas-Centaur rocket. On June 2, 1966, it successfully soft-landed on the dusty plains of the lunar region known as the Ocean of Storms. The Surveyor probe stood 10 feet high on its three landing legs, was 14 feet across, and weighed 2,194 lbs. Its TV cameras transmitted over 11,000 pictures that provided valuable information about the characteristics of the Moon's surface. Over the next two years six more Surveyor space probes were launched to different regions of the Moon. They proved essential in mapping out future landing sites for the Apollo program.

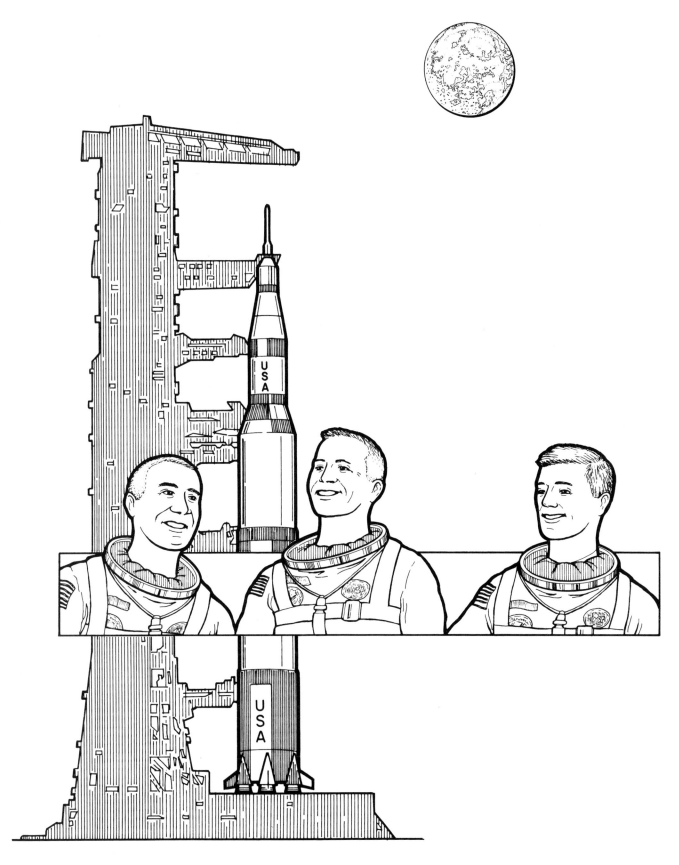

Grissom, White, and Chaffee. In January 1967 the United States suffered the first loss of life in its space-exploration program. Astronauts Virgil "Gus" Grissom, Edward White, and Roger Chaffee died in a flash fire during ground testing of their Apollo command module. An electrical spark ignited in the pure oxygen environment of the space capsule and the three died within seconds. The nation mourned the deaths of the astronauts and NASA took steps to remedy the cause of the fire. The possibility of danger or loss of life had always been understood and accepted by the astronauts. They believed that the risk involved was justified by the quest for knowledge and the expansion of the human frontier into space. We salute their courage and commitment and will remember them as true American heroes.

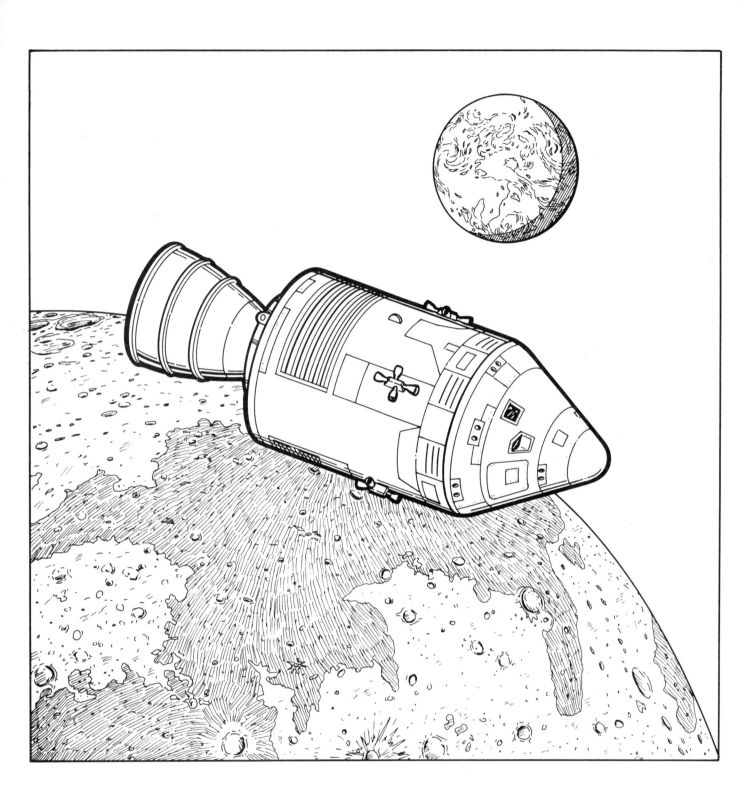

Apollo 8. In 1968 the American goal of reaching the Moon was in sight. The Apollo program to send three men to the Moon, land two of them, and then return safely, was underway. The Apollo spaceship would be launched by the 363-foot-high, 3,000-ton Saturn V. This multistage rocket generated enough thrust to propel the Apollo to 25,000 mph on its voyage to the Moon 246,000 miles away. The Apollo spacecraft consisted of three sections. First was the Command Module, in which the astronauts rode to and from the Moon; next, the Service Module, which contained their power and life-support systems; finally, the Lunar Module, the ship that would take them from lunar orbit down to the surface and back up again.

On December 21, 1968, Apollo 8 (minus the Lunar Module) was launched with William Anders, Frank Borman, and James Lovell, Jr. as the crew. They reached the Moon on December 24, 1968, completing ten lunar orbits in 20 hours at an altitude of 70 miles, the first human beings to directly view the far side of the Moon. While circling the Moon they gave a dramatic Christmas Eve greeting to the people of the world. They were returned safely to Earth on December 27 after a journey lasting 147 hours. This historic achievement would, however, soon be overshadowed by the most important event in the history of space exploration, the first actual landing of men on the Moon.

Lunar Rover. The Lunar Rover was a "Moonmobile" used on the later Apollo moon flights. It was attached to the side of the Lunar Module during landing and released by pulling several restraining cords. The Lunar Rover was 10 feet long and 6 feet wide, and weighed 460 lbs. Powered by an electric battery, it had a top speed of 8½ mph and a range of 57 miles, and had tires made of wire mesh. During the Apollo 15 mission the astronauts drove it to the Hadley Rille region, a distance of 18 miles. They drove 16 miles to the Descartes crater on Apollo 16, and on Apollo 17 drove 22 miles to the Taurus Littrow region. The Lunar Rover had a large dish antenna that allowed direct communication with Earth. The TV camera on the Lunar Rover was used to televise the lift-off of the Lunar Excursion Module as it blasted back into orbit to link up with the Command Module. The Lunar Rover was a valuable tool for collecting rock samples and for reaching different areas of the Moon. All three Lunar Rovers were left on the Moon and can be reenergized and used again by future astronauts.

Apollo 11. On July 20, 1969, for the first time in history, a human being set foot on another planetary body, Earth's natural satellite, the Moon. An estimated television audience of 500 million people watched as American astronaut Neil A. Armstrong stepped off his bug-like Lunar Module and said, "That's one small step for a man, one giant leap for mankind."

The astronauts selected for the historic Apollo 11 mission were Neil Armstrong, Edwin "Buzz" Aldrin, and Michael Collins. Armstrong was an ex-Navy pilot and NASA test pilot. Buzz Aldrin was an Air Force Colonel, graduate of West Point, Korean War combat pilot, and astrophysics PhD. Michael Collins was an Air Force Lt. Colonel and West Point graduate. They were launched on July 16, 1969 by a Saturn V rocket and achieved lunar orbit on July 20. Armstrong and Aldrin descended to the surface in the Lunar Module while Collins remained with the Command Module in a parking orbit.

They stayed on the surface for 21 hours, collecting rocks, conducting experiments, and taking photographs. Their spacesuits had 21 layers of fiberglass designed to withstand the vacuum of space, extremes of heat and cold, and micrometeors. After blasting off from their landing site they rejoined Collins in the Command ship and returned to Earth on July 24 to a heroes' welcome. The Apollo program continued on to Apollo 17 in 1972, advancing our knowledge of the Moon and space travel immensely. Among the instruments and debris left on the Moon was a stainless steel plaque conveying the highest aspirations of space exploration in a simple but eloquent statement, "We came in peace for all Mankind."

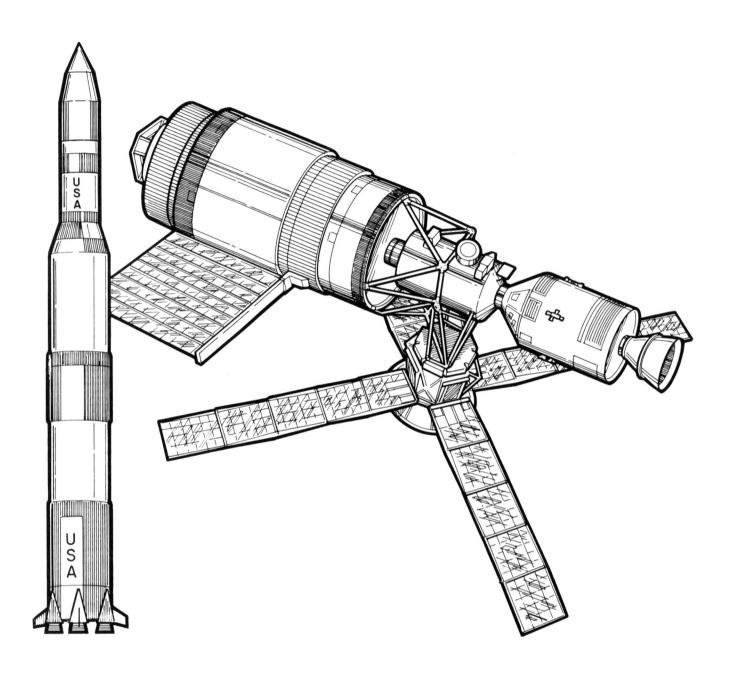

Skylab 1. The final part of the Apollo program was the launching of the Skylab manned space station. It was boosted into orbit by a Saturn V rocket *(left)* on May 14, 1973. Its main lab section was actually derived from the 48-foot fourth stage of the Saturn V. The first crew arrived on May 25 and had to effect an immediate repair on the space station. During the ascent into orbit, a portion of the lab's solar heat shield was torn away, as well as one of its main solar power panels. Without this thermal shield, temperatures inside Skylab climbed to 165 degrees, making it uninhabitable. Working outside in their space suits, the astronauts set up a replacement heat shield and saved the mission from failure. The space lab consisted of a 17-foot-long docking module, an instrument unit, the main lab and crew quarters, and various antennae and solar power panels. It totaled 118 feet in length and weighed 200,000 lbs. It was manned by three different crews between May 1973 and February 1974 who spent a total of 172 days in space. The astronauts carried out many scientific experiments vital to our knowledge of living in the environment of outer space.

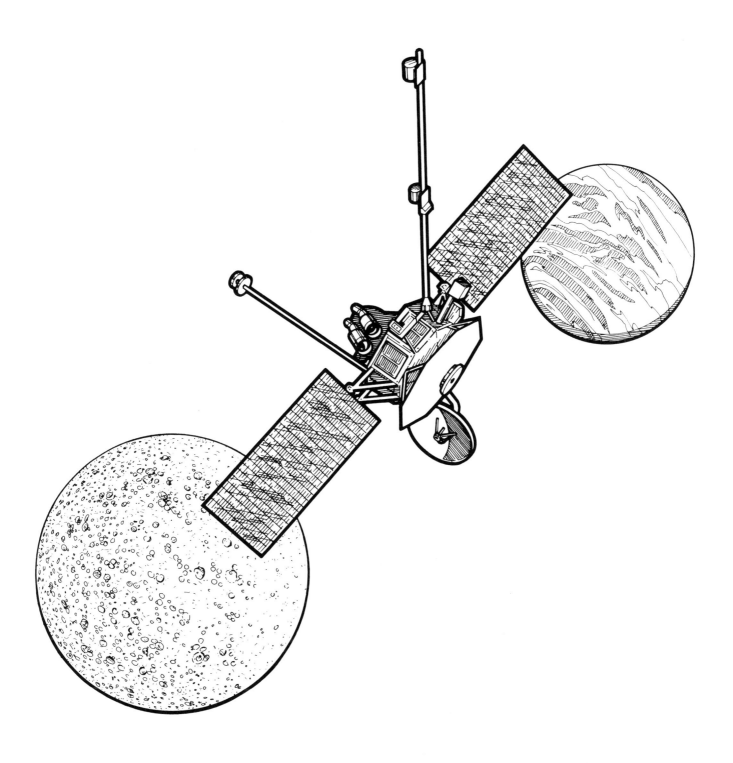

Mariner 10 Probe to Venus and Mercury. The last in the Mariner series of space probes was Mariner 10. It was designed to flyby and photograph the planets Venus and Mercury. It was launched in November 1973 by an Atlas-Centaur rocket and reached Venus in February 1974. It passed within 3,600 miles of the planet and returned over 3,500 pictures. It flew on past Venus and encountered Mercury in March 1974, coming as close as 430 miles. It found that Mercury had no atmosphere and that its surface was heavily cratered and cracked. Its temperature on the Sun-facing side was over 800 degrees F. and on its dark side dipped to –300 degrees F. The Mariner robot probes were very successful and added immensely to our knowledge of the planets in our Solar System.

Skylab 4. The last crew of the Skylab space station set a long-duration space-flight record for American astronauts. The crew consisted of Gerald Carr, Edward Gibson, and Bill Pogue. They spent a total of 84 days in space conducting experiments, giving science demonstrations, and photographing the Earth and Sun. They returned to Earth in their Apollo spaceship in February 1974.

Skylab was intended to be reoccupied with the start of the Space Shuttle program but nature intervened. Unusual sunspot activity in 1978 had produced a temporary expansion of the Earth's atmosphere. This created a drag on Skylab and its orbit began to decay. It fell from orbit in July 1979, burning up as it plunged through the atmosphere and scattering debris along a 2400-mile track including the Indian Ocean and Western Australia. With the end of the Skylab program, the first phase of America's manned space efforts came to a close. Mercury, Gemini, Apollo, and Skylab had all proven very successful in providing a foundation for the continuing exploration of space. The next phase would soon begin with the world's first reusable spaceship, the Space Shuttle.

Apollo 18–Soyuz 19 Linkup. Eighteen months after the last Skylab crew completed their mission, the Apollo spaceship made its final flight. Apollo 18 was launched into orbit to rendezvous and dock with the Soviet Soyuz 19 spacecraft in a dramatic gesture of American–Soviet goodwill and co-operation. The Soviet Soyuz was launched first on July 15, 1975, by an A-2/SL-4 rocket. Seven hours later the Apollo was launched by the Saturn 1B. After several hours of maneuvering, the two ships linked up in an orbit 140 miles high. The American astronauts were Tom Stafford, Deke Slayton, and Vance Brand. The Soviet cosmonauts were Alexei Leonov and Valery Kubasov. They spent 44 hours in orbit together, exchanging toasts and gifts, and visiting each other's spacecraft. On July 21 the Soviet crew disconnected from the Apollo and returned to Earth. The American crew stayed in orbit for three more days, returning on July 24. The Apollo–Soyuz linkup was an important symbol of international cooperation and may be regarded as a model for future Soviet–American space missions.

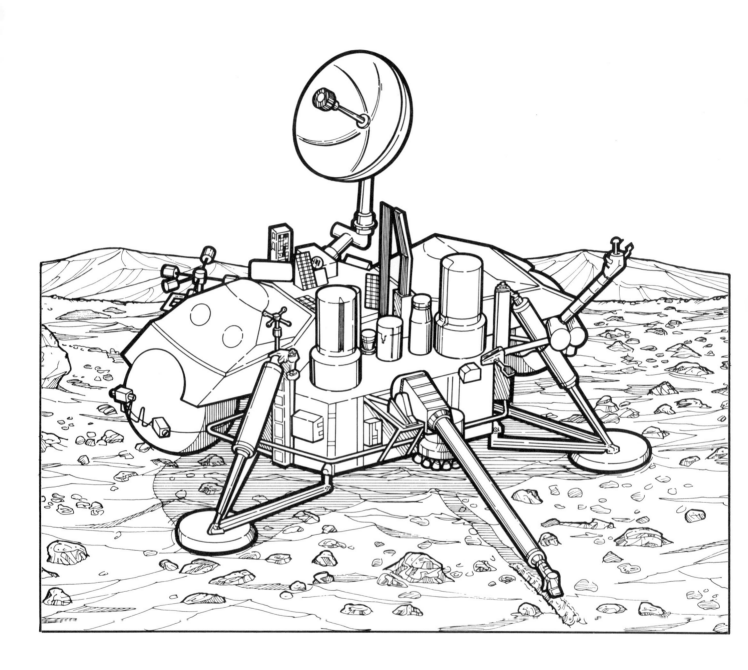

Viking 1 and 2 Mars Probes. One of the most ambitious planetary exploration missions was conducted by twin American Mars probes, Viking 1 and 2 (launched by Titan IIIC rockets). Viking 1 was launched in August 1975, touching down on the Martian surface on July 20, 1976, and transmitting photos from the Plains of Gold. Viking 2 was launched in September 1975 and landed in September 1976, on the Utopia Plains. The Vikings were equipped with a formidable array of instruments, the most remarkable being a self-contained biology lab for testing soil samples retrieved by a remote-control digger arm. The Vikings found that temperature on Mars ranges from 50 degrees F. at noon to −225 at night, and provided data suggesting that Mars had

once been much warmer, with a thicker atmosphere and rivers of water. They found an atmosphere containing all the elements for life (including oxygen, nitrogen, carbon, and water vapor), but in amounts too small to sustain known forms. They found that Martian skies are peach-colored because of suspended red-orange soil particles, and that Martian soil is reddish because of the presence of iron oxide (rust). Certain reactions were recorded by the biology lab that suggested organic or lifelike activity. The results of these tests were inconclusive in solving the question of life on Mars. The final answer may have to wait for future robot probes or the astronauts who will eventually walk on the Martian surface.

Voyager 1 and 2 Deep Space Probes. The most successful American unmanned planetary probes are the twin Voyagers still operating in deep space. Their primary mission was to explore Jupiter, Saturn, Uranus, Neptune, and their numerous Moons. They were 14 feet in diameter and 12 feet high, weighed 1,797 lbs, and were launched by the Titan IIIC. Power was supplied by onboard nuclear generators They were equipped with high-resolution TV cameras and a large dish antenna to transmit data back to Earth. Voyager 1 was launched on September 5, 1977, and encountered Jupiter in March 1979, passing within 177,000 miles. It revealed that the Great Red Spot is a centuries-old storm system 20,000 miles in diameter. In November 1980 it flew by Saturn at a distance of 77,000 miles, photographing its ring system of dust, rocks, and ice. Voyager 1 left our Solar System in 1980 and entered interstellar space.

On August 20, 1977, Voyager 2 was launched, reaching Jupiter in July 1979, passing within 390,000 miles. Its flyby of Saturn occurred in August 1981, at a distance of 63,000 miles. During its encounter with these planets Voyager also photographed their satellites (Jupiter had 15 and Saturn 23!), "capturing" volcanic eruptions on Jupiter's moon Io, and flying within 2,500 miles of Titan—a moon of Saturn larger than the planet Mercury, with a thick atmosphere (mostly nitrogen like Earth's). In January 1986 Voyager 2 took the first close-up photos of Uranus. It confirmed Earth-based observations that Uranus has a ring system like Saturn's, though smaller and less colorful. Voyager 2 was scheduled to encounter Neptune in August 1989 before leaving the Solar System. The Voyagers will transmit data back to Earth until the year 2007, when they will be over nine billion miles from Earth.

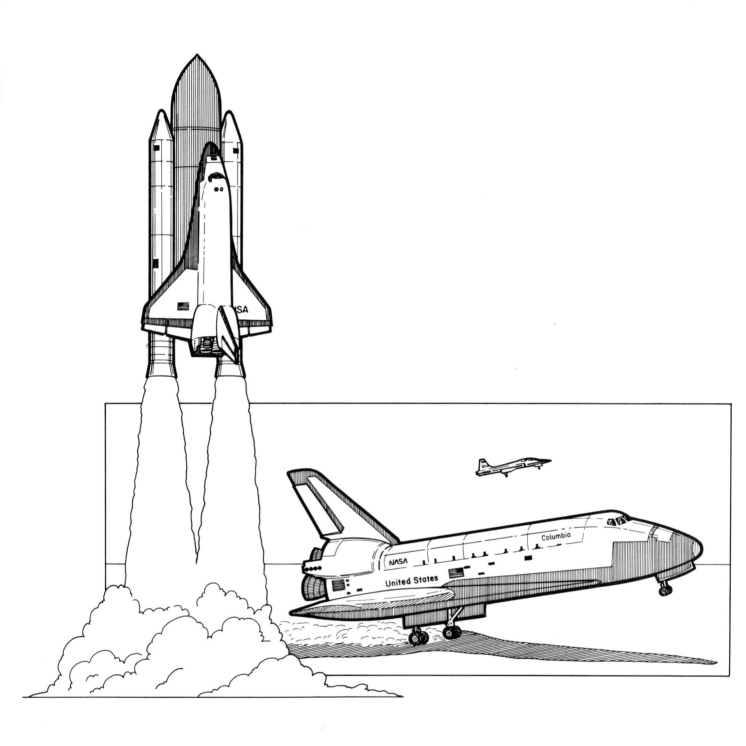

STS-1 *Columbia* Test Flight. In April 1981 the United States began a new phase of its manned space program with the Space Shuttle Transportation System (STS). It is a winged spaceship designed to be launched into orbit by rocket power and then glide back to Earth to be flown again. Its primary purpose is to launch satellites and scientific cargo, and assist in the construction of permanently occupied space stations. The Space Shuttle consists of a main ship (the Orbiter), two 148' solid-fuel rocket boosters, and a central external fuel tank for the three engines of the Orbiter. The Orbiter is a delta-winged craft, 122 feet long with a 78-foot wingspan, and weighs 152,000 lbs. It has a 15' × 60' cargo bay and can carry a cargo weighing up to 65,000 lbs. Its three main engines are powered by liquid oxygen and liquid hydrogen. The skin of the Orbiter is covered with silica tiles to absorb the intense heat of reentry. The white tiles can withstand temperatures up to 1,200 degrees F., and the black tiles up to 2,300 degrees. On April 2, 1981, Robert Crippen and John Young were launched into orbit on the Flight of STS-1, the Space Shuttle *Columbia*. They spent two days in orbit and landed at Edwards Air Force Base in California.

Salyut 7. Since 1971 the Soviet Union has launched a series of small manned space stations called Salyut ("salute"). In the spring of 1982 they launched the Salyut 7 *(left)* into an orbit 130 miles above the Earth. The cosmonauts docked with the space station in a Soyuz-T space-ferry vehicle. The Salyut 7 lab was 50 feet long and 14 feet wide, and weighed 55,000 lbs. It had docking ports for Soyuz vehicles at both ends. During the mission of Salyut 7 cosmonauts Anatoli Bereovoi and Valentin Lebedev set an all-time endurance record of 211 days in space. They were visited by other teams of cosmonauts (including the second woman to enter space, Svetlana Savitskaya) and were resupplied by Progress supply ships, unmanned versions of the Soyuz. The Soyuz *(right)* consists of a spherical orbiting module with a docking probe, a cup-shaped descent module for landing, and a cylindrical instrument unit with fold-out solar panels. It is 26 feet long and weighs 15,000 lbs. At this time the U.S.S.R. has a modified version of the Salyut in orbit called Mir ("peace"). It has ports for six Soyuz vehicles and is manned by teams of cosmonauts on a continuing basis.

***Columbia* Mission STS-5.** The Space Shuttle *Columbia* began its first operational flight on November 11, 1982 with the STS-5 mission. The crew stayed in space for five days and completed 81 orbits. During that time the astronauts launched two satellites from the cargo bay, an American SBS-C and a Canadian Anik C-3. The satellites were deployed spinning at 50 rpm for stability. After they were a safe distance from the Shuttle, their own rocket motors ignited and boosted them to a geosynchronous orbit 22,300 miles above the Earth. *Columbia* had performed the first of many missions and would be followed by its sister ships, *Challenger, Discovery,* and *Atlantis.*

Sally Ride. On June 18, 1983, America's first woman astronaut rode into space aboard the Shuttle *Challenger*. Dr. Sally K. Ride was a Mission Specialist, an astronaut trained to perform specific scientific duties during the flight. Dr. Ride had an extensive background in science before her selection for the astronaut program. She earned two bachelor's degrees from Stanford University, one in astrophysics and one in English literature. She later went on to attain a master's and PhD. degree in astrophysics from Stanford.

On board the *Challenger* Dr. Ride was responsible for testing and utilizing the 50'-long Remote Manipulator Arm that she had helped develop. This jointed robot arm was designed to retrieve faulty satellites and place them in the Shuttle cargo bay for repair or return to Earth. To be selected from over 8,900 astronaut applicants and finally chosen to be America's first woman in space reflects Sally Ride's dedication and ability.

Manned Maneuvering Unit. On mission 41-B of the Shuttle *Challenger*, the first test of the Manned Manuevering Unit or MMU was conducted. On February 7, 1984, Bruce McCandless became the first astronaut to free-fly in space, unconnected by a tether line to his spacecraft. The MMU is a backpack worn over the regular life-support system on the astronaut's back. It has 24 nozzles that release compressed nitrogen gas, allowing an astronaut to propel himself forward, backward, sideways, up, and down, and even do a somersault. The MMU has enough compressed gas for a six-hour space walk. With the availability of the MMU, astronauts have far greater freedom to move about and work in space than with the previous tether-line system. This will become increasingly important when construction of the large, permanently occupied American space station begins in the 1990s. The astronauts will be required to work in space over longer periods of time and perform more complex construction tasks, and the MMU will play a key role in those duties.

***Challenger* Mission 41-C.** *Challenger* mission 41-C took place in April 1984. During the flight, American astronauts recovered a defective satellite and repaired it in the Shuttle's cargo bay. The Solar Max satellite was retrieved by the Remote Manipulator Arm, a 50-foot-long jointed robot arm that was operated from within the crew cabin. The Solar Max was 13 feet long, weighed 5,000 lbs., and was deployed to study the Sun. Astronauts George Nelson and James van Hoften repaired the satellite after seven hours of working in

their spacesuits in the open cargo bay. The crew also released the Long Duration Exposure Facility. This was a 30-foot-long, 12-sided cylinder containing 57 experiments to measure the effects of long-term exposure to the harshness of outer space. It was the largest shuttle payload carried, weighing in at 21,500 lbs. It was designated to be retrieved after one year in space but it is still in orbit. It is scheduled to be picked up and brought back to Earth on an upcoming Shuttle flight.

The *Challenger* Tragedy. On January 28, 1986, the United States experienced the worst disaster in the history of manned space flight. The Space Shuttle *Challenger* exploded 74 seconds after lift-off and all seven crew members died. People around the world were stunned and saddened by this unexpected loss. America will always remember the *Challenger* heroes: Michael Smith, Francis (Dick) Scobee, Ronald MacNair, Ellison Onizuka, Christa McAuliffe, Gregory Jarvis, and Judith Resnick. Their dedication and commitment to the dream of space exploration will inspire us in the years to come. The finest tribute we can pay them is to rededicate ourselves to the challenge of discovery in the frontier of space.